1976 - 2006   Adamson, Christopher THE ROAD TO JEWEL BEACH (2004) • Amichai, Yehuda and Yannis Ritsos TRAVELS OF A LATTER-DAY BENJAMIN OF TUDELA and HELEN/Exile Editions Number 2 (1976) • Amichai, Yehuda TRAVELS (1986) • Amprimoz, Alexandre TOO MANY POPES (1990) • Annesley, David THE ANNESLEY DRAWINGS (1980) • Archambault Théatre Collective NO BIG DEAL! (1982) • Aude THE INDISCERNIBLE MOVEMENT (1998); THE WHOLE MAN (2000); HUMAN (2006) • Bacque, James OUR FATHERS' WAR (2006) • Baguinho, Edith ODE TO TIO CALICO AND TIA DORES (1997) • Barlow, John SAFE TELEPATHY (1996); ASHINEOVSUN (1999); ASHINEOVSUN II (2002) • Beaulieu, Michel SPELLS OF FURY (1984); COUNTENANCES (1986); KALEIDOSCOPE: Perils of a Solemn Body (1998) • Beaulieu, Victor-Lévy A QUÉBÉCOIS DREAM (1978, 1988); JOS CONNAISANT (1982); SATAN BELHUMEUR (1983); STEVEN Le HÉRAULT (1987) • Bessette, Gérard NOT FOR EVERY EYE (1984); INCUBATION (1986); THE CYCLE (1987) • Blais, Marie-Claire THE OCEAN/Exile Editions Number 6 (1977) • Boissonneau, Alice THERE WILL BE GARDENS A Memoir of Two-Storey Dreams in a City (1991); A SUDDEN BRIGHTNESS (1994) • Böszörményi, Zoltán FAR FROM NOTHING (2006) • Bramer, Shannon SUITCASES AND OTHER POEMS (1999); SCARF (2001) • Brault, Jacques FRAGILE MOMENTS (1985); ON THE ROAD NO MORE (1993) • Brett, Brian ALLEGORIES OF LOVE AND DISASTER (1993); UPROAR'S YOUR ONLY MUSIC New Poems & A Memoir (2004) • Callaghan, Barry AS CLOSE AS WE CAME (1982); STONE BLIND LOVE (1988) • Callaghan, Barry (With an editorial introduction) LORDS OF WINTER AND OF LOVE: A Book of Canadian Love Poems in English and French (1983); CANADIAN TRAVELLERS IN ITALY (1989); EXILE: THE FIRST FIFTEEN YEARS Volumes 1-3 (1992); THIS AIN'T NO HEALING TOWN Toronto Stories (1995); WE WASN'T PALS: Poetry and Prose of the First World War (2001); YOUNG BLOODS: Stories from Exile, 1972-2001 (2001); IRREALITIES, LACONICS & SONNETS/W.W.E Ross (2003) • Callaghan, Morley SEASON OF THE WITCH: A Play/Exile Editions Number 3 (1976); THE NEW YORKER STORIES (2001); THAT SUMMER IN PARIS (2002); THE COMPLETE STORIES Volume One/Volume Two/Volume Three/Volume Four (2003); IT'S NEVER OVER (2004); STRANGE FUGITIVE (2004); A TIME FOR JUDAS (2005); THE VOW (2005) • Camilleri, MaryAnn LADIES, PLEASE! A Drag View of the Nineties (1994) • Carberry, Colin THE GREEN TABLE (2003) • Cavalli, Patrizia MY POEMS WILL NOT CHANGE THE WORLD Selected Poems 1974-1992 (1998) • Clark, John Livingstone PRAYERS AND OTHER UNFINISHED LETTERS (1995); PASSAGE TO INDIGO AND OTHER POEMS (1996); BACK TO BETHANY; Eigthy-nine Paragraphs about Jesus and Lazarus in Abbotsford (1997); BODY AND SOUL New and Selected Poems (2002) • Clarke, Austin IN THIS CITY Short Stories (1992); THERE ARE NO ELDERS Short Stories (1993); A PASSAGE BACK HOME A Personal Reminiscence of Samuel Selvon (1994); THE PRIME MINISTER (1994); THE AUSTIN CLARKE READER (1996) • Clarke, James SILVER MERCIES (1997); THE RAGGEDY PARADE (1998); THE ANCIENT PEDIGREES OF PLUMS (1999); THE WAY EVERYONE IS INSIDE (2000); FLYING HOME THROUGH THE DARK (2001); HOW TO BRIBE A JUDGE Poems From the Bench (2002); FORCED PASSAGE (2005) • Couzyn, Jeni THE SELECTED POETRY OF JENI COUZYN (2000) • Curtin, Walter CURTIN CALL: A Photographer's Candid View of 25 Years of Music in Canada (1994) • D'Alfonso, Antonio GETTING ON WITH POLITICS (2002); A FRIDAY IN AUGUST (2005); GAMBLING WITH FAILURE (2005) • Dault, Gary Michael FLYING FISH AND OTHER POEMS (1996) • Day, David GOTHIC (1986); JUST SAY 'NO' TO FAMILY VALUES And Other Rants, Howls and Moans (1997) • De, Claire DESIRE AS NATURAL DISASTER (1995); SOUNDLESS LOVES (1996); THE SPARROW HAS CUT THE DAY IN HALF (1998) • Delius, Friedrich Christian THE PEARS OF RIBBECK (1991) • Dodic, N.J. THE MADNESS OF HISTORY (1994) • Drach, Ivan ORCHARD LAMPS (1989); THE MADONNA OF CHERNOBYL AND Other Poems (1992) • Ducharme, Réjean HA! HA! (1986) • Ellenwood, Ray EGREGORE: THE MONTRÉAL AUTOMATIST MOVEMENT (1992) • Ellenwood, Ray (As Translator) TOTAL REFUSAL: The Complete 1948 Manifesto of the Montréal Automatists (1985, 1998, 2001) • Etrog, Sorel DREAM CHAMBER Joyce and the DaDa Circus: A Collage (1986); IMAGES FROM THE FILM SPIRAL (1987) • Ferron, Jacques THE CART (1980, 1988); THE PENNILESS REDEEMER (1984); PAPA BOSS, QUINCE JAM (1992) • Gauvreau, Claude ENTRAILS (1991); THE CHARGE OF THE EXPORMYABLE MOOSE (1996) • Gibson, Margaret THE FEAR ROOM and Other Stories (1996); DESERT THIRST (1997) • Giguere, Roland ROSE & THORN (1988) • Glickman, Darren THE WEIGHT OF THE WORLD AND OTHER STORIES (1999) • Gorjup, Branko (As Editor) WHITE GLOVES OF THE DOORMAN The Works of Leon Rooke (2004) • Gotlieb, Phyllis RED BLOOD BLACK INK WHITE PAPER New and Selected Poems 1961-2001 (2002) • Gould, Martha POEMS FOR OWEN (1997); WITH WHALES IN THE WATER (1997) • Guriel, Jason TECHNICOLOURED (2006) • Graham, Hugh WHERE THE SUN DON'T SHINE (2000); PLOUGHING THE SEAS: The Nicaraguan Resistance and the CIA in the Jungles of Southern Nicaragua 1984-1987 (2001) • Hanley, James THE GERMAN PRISONER (2006) • Harvey, Kenneth J. KILL THE POETS: Anti-Verse (1995); THE GREAT MISOGYNIST (1996); EVERYONE HATES A BEAUTY QUEEN Provocative Opinions and Irreverent Humor (1998) • Hayward, Steven BUDDHA STEVENS AND OTHER STORIES (2000) • Hénault, Gilles SIGNALS FOR SEERS (1988) • Holoborodko, Vasyl ICARUS WITH BUTTERFLY WINGS & OTHER POEMS (1991) • Jeffrey, Lawrence FOUR PLAYS (1992); WHO LOOK IN STOVE (1993) • Kalynets, Ihor CROWNING THE SCARECROW Appeals to Conscience in Lviv 1968-1969 Selected Poems (1990) • Keating, Diane NO BIRDS OR FLOWERS (1982); THE OPTIC HEART (1984); THE YEAR ONE New and Selected Poems (2001) • Keefer, Janice Kulyk MIDNIGHT STROLL (2006) • Knister, Raymond AFTER EXILE A Raymond Knister Poetry Reader (2003) • Lane, Patrick MORTAL REMAINS (1992, 1999) • Lapointe, Paul-Marie THE 5TH SEASON (1985) • Lawrence, P. Scott AROUND THE MULBERRY TREE (1984) • Lawson, JonArno ; LOVE IS AN OBSERVANT TRAVELLER (1997); INKLINGS (1999) • Lilburn, Tim TOURIST TO ECSTASY (1989) • Lynch, William CLOUDS: A NOVEL (1999) • MacEwen, Gwendolyn THE TROJAN WOMEN The Trojan Women by Euripides and Helen and Orestes by Ritsos (1990); THE BIRDS After the Play of Aristophanes (1993); THE POETRY OF GWENDOLYN MACEWEN Two Volumes (1993) • Marteau, Robert ATLANTE (1979); PENTECOST (1979); TREATISE ON WHITE AND TINCTURE (1979); INTERLUDE (1982); MOUNT ROYAL (1982); PIG-SKINNING (1984); RIVER WITHOUT END: A Log Book of the Saint Lawrence (1987); VOYAGE TO VENDÉE (1987); EIDOLON TWO LONG POEMS Treatise On White and Tincture and Atlante (1990); VENICE AT HER MIRROR (1991) • McDevitt, Neale ONE DAY EVEN TREVI WILL CRUMBLE (2002) • McGee, Thomas D'Arcy THOMAS D'ARCY McGEE Selected Verse(1991) • McLaughlin, JoAnne THE BANSHEE DIARIES (1998) • Meigs, Mary ILLUSTRATIONS FOR TWO NOVELS BY MARIE-CLAIRE BLAIS/Exile Editions Number 5 (1977) • Meyer, Bruce ANYWHERE (2000); THE SPIRIT OF THE BRIDE (2002); OCEANS (2004) • Meyer, Bruce (As Editor, in collaboration with Barry Callaghan) SELECTED POEMS OF FRANK PREWETT (1987); WE WASN'T PALS Canadian Poetry and Prose of the First World War (2001) • Mihalič, Slavko BLACK APPLES Selected Poems 1954-1987 (1989) • Montague, John THE DEAD KINGDOM (1984); THE LOVE POEM: MOUNT EAGLE (1989); AN OCCASION OF SIN Short stories (1992); SELECTED POEMS (1982, 1992) •

TECHNICOLORED

TECHNICOLORED

JASON GURIEL

TORONTO

Exile Editions
2006

First published in Canada in 2006 by
Exile Editions Ltd.
20 Dale Avenue
Toronto, Ontario, M4W 1K4
telephone: 416 485 9468
www.ExileEditions.com

Library and Archives Canada Cataloguing in Publication

Guriel, Jason 1978 -

   Technicolored / Jason Guriel.

Poems.

ISBN 1-55096-003-2

   I. Title.

PS8613.U74T43 2006   C811'.6   C2006-902271-2

Design and Composition: Gabriela Campos
Cover Photograph: Joe Paczuski
Typesetting: Moons of Jupiter
Printed in Canada: Gauvin Imprimerie

The publisher would like to acknowledge the financial
assistance of The Canada Council for the Arts.

 Conseil des Arts   Canada Council
          du Canada   for the Arts

Sales Distribution:
McArthur & Company c/o Harper Collins
1995 Markham Road, Toronto, ON M1B 5M8
toll free: 1 800 387 0117   fax: 1 800 668 5788

Variations of these poems first appeared in the following: *The Antigonish Review*: "As She Lay in Her Bathtub, Holding a Flute of Wine"; *Arc*: "Accidental Poetry Written by My Father," "Envy for an Impostor"; *CV2*: "The Day Frank O'Hara Died. Detail."; *The Dalhousie Review*: "The Question"; *Descant*: "The Lady from Shanghai Shows Another Side," "Eleventh Hour Instructions to a Prize Poodle"; *Exile*: "Fellini's Whore Executes the Rumba," "*Rififi*," "Ennui at the Kissing Booth in B&W," "Ricky's Twin Bed Addresses Lucy's," "An Old Cello Addresses Its Young Trophy Bow," "On Decadence," "Mining Accident in Alberta: A Maimed Sonnet," "Motel Art. Detail.," "Appreciating Female Form, 1960," "On Behalf of All Instructive Images," "Orson Welles' Smile," "Ava Gardner Responds to 'Ava Gardner Reincarnated as a Magnolia' by Margaret Atwood," "A Dust Mote Addresses the Digital Divide," "A Two-night DVD Rental Rebuts," "Memorabilia," "Antigonus' Grievance," "For Weldon Kees as He Teeters"; *The Fiddlehead*: "Elegy for Josef Hassid (1923-1950)"; *Grain*: "As Suggested by the Calculations of Copernicus"; *The Malahat Review*: "Audrey Hepburn's Right Hand," "To Keep Jimmy Stewart"; *The Nashwaak Review*: "Trouty," "As We Dolly Back," "On-set in Hades, 1911"; *Other Voices*: "The Score"; PRISM: "Autumn at the End of *The Third Man*," "Cleaning Kill in the Kitchen at Midnight, Father Made a Good Point," "Rosebud"; *Taddle Creek*: "*Contempt*," "Some Kind of a Man."

My thanks to *all* the Editors . . .

To my father, the Hungarian
who stood in our stairwell
day after day, tuning a violin,
I owe you the best silence I can manage.

To my mother, the woman from
Newfoundland who christened
fried slices of bologna, "Mexican hats,"
I owe you a metaphor.

CONTENTS

The Vitascope, the first practical projector, dates only from 1901, so viewing moving pictures had just become possible. Can we recover the freshness of [Ernest] Fenollosa's pioneer analogy? In "things" he saw "cross-sections cut through actions, snap-shots"; likewise in single ideograms and single cinema frames. Both exist for the sake of their blended succession, the moving picture, the sentence, the poetic line.

—HUGH KENNER

Rosy-fingered dawn, my ass.
This show's in Technicolor.

—AUGUST KLEINZAHLER

A DUST MOTE ADDRESSES THE DIGITAL DIVIDE

Swirling in the projector's beam,
I circulate onscreen
through the skin of Bette Davis:
a nomadic mole
or rogue freckle,
expelled from the society
of its famous face—

an artist, then, rendering
my beam visible
the way rain stipples
a Duesy's headlamps,
each drop's curve positing
a hemisphere on which
light might pause.

You want me Remastered,
the reels dismantled,
film stock scoured clean.
But isn't Bette's complexion
planed of imperfections
now perfectly plain?
Look up: any moment this beam—
my medium—might curl
to fashion your halo.

In the hall of mirrors, Rita Hayworth aims
her pistol at the Irishman. To her immediate
left, another Rita also aims a pistol, also
at an Irishman. And another Rita, her
pistol aimed, and another Rita, her
pistol aimed, and so on, and on—

an infinity of Ritas, shoulder-to-shoulder,
ordered like some column of soldiers,
hair styled chic and short, serving
the same threat—too many Ritas, really,
plotted like an equation's points, curving
off and away into ungraphed darkness.

And as her husband, the famous barrister, steps
out of the shadows—as a thousand famous barristers
step out of the shadows, as a million, as they, too,
aim pistols, a million pistols at a million Ritas,

the hall of mirrors holds its breath...

To see the breaking of that much glass,
the Irishman reflects, would be something.
But to get finally to the bottom of women?
Now that would be something.

FELLINI'S WHORE EXECUTES THE RUMBA

Ask Penelope, surrounded by that gaggle of suitors:
there are worse ways to spend a life
than waiting patiently for an epic to advance.

Saraghina, for example, sat on a wooden chair
that faced ocean, and wondered whether
a great mythology could ever
collect against some unsuspecting sail
and blow an Odysseus by her beach.

And one day, a few young boys reached
Saraghina, but not by boat. They came
on foot from a nearby town, following shoreline,
and wanted the rumba rubbed all over their eyes.

For coins, Saraghina would dance,
there being worse ways to spend a life, after all,
than waiting patiently for an epic to advance.

Think this skin scandalous?
Some scrapes aren't so easily rouged,
and anyway, you're only every john
who's ever left my gleam face-
down on top of his TV,
a laugh track rumbling beneath
like intestinal tract working
some gristle. Granted,
most smudges wipe off,
but look at me: this over-skated
pond on which no beam
finds footing; a scuffed coaster
bearing your Budweiser.
At least Beta players had teeth
and (in *Videodrome*) a heartbeat,
a mile of magnetic soul, unspooled.
Who, then, wouldn't want to be
tape chewed by your VCR,
free from fingerprints?

TO KEEP JIMMY STEWART

I

Ladies, Kim Novak needs no bouquet
and knows this, leaves it
to bloom on the bench.
Seated in a gallery,
she lets the paintings
linger over her, the oils in awe.
A man could lose both eyes
in her Technicolored
hair, blonde and
curling into
its bun
like
a spiral-
ing staircase,
like water circling its
drain. A man could lose balance.

2

In fact, was there ever a better body
to tail to the edge
of San Francisco Bay?
Suicides, take a cue from Kim
and be beautiful about it
(you're not heaving some sack
into the water). And keep
Jimmy Stewart in the corner
of your eye. You will want him
diving in, will want saving—
to wake naked with immunity
between a stranger's sheets,
to try red against your skin.
Go on. Show a fireplace how to smoulder.

3

Above all, keep him comfortable
or keep him crippled—just
keep Jimmy Stewart.
Glide with Grace
Kelly, and impoverish
every square inch of his apartment.
Your dress should claim a race
(French) and live but one day
on the body, darkening
like a lampshade when subtracted
from your bright curves.
So climb a killer's fire escape
if you must, but please,
do it in couture.

4

When he nods off, ladies
put aside books about the Himalayas
and part only the pages of *Bazaar*.
When men nod off, women
smile wickedly.

She knows what her lineup of men
passing around pieces of gum
has secretly hoped it could purchase today.

Therefore, the dark-haired girl
tasting like the orange
bestowed earlier by a fiancé

now tips her body towards me
and slips between my teeth a tongue
unsanctioned by any fair

before returning her attention
to the town library's only edition of Rimbaud
with the sneaky French on the facing pages.

Note that I've never asked
upon how many strings you've played,
were they better than me, more taut,
did they make a different sound
when you laid your young weight across them.

My noises, you'll find competent and dignified,
sombre as the cobblestone square
where I was, in my youth,
often played between the legs of a prodigy
while pigeons scanned feet—falling like trochees—
and flung wishes minted themselves
in fountain water.

ON DECADENCE

The dull months are strolled through
easily enough. But every so often you
slip on a week that's slick
as a Roman bath, and a girl you
wouldn't even bother your dreams with
has her magnificent way with you.

A week: six or seven exquisite days
plucked as if from a stem and
urged on your startled lips like grapes.
You admit them, and an impractical appetite,
one you weren't even aware of,
is fed though not sustained—
an airy, spacious appetite that cannot,
like the big top, simply collapse and fold.

Still, what a wonder you are, finally.
At least for a week, your sex is accomplished.
You're the Caligula you couldn't have been,
clawing just any leg in public (Malcolm
McDowell in Tinto's tawdry turkey) though
one wonders how you'll now
return to sensible living.

Bored, this girl, you suspect, will resume
better sex with unexpended exes.
Her life story's treatment, lush and intricate,
clings to the issue of her body like red fishnet.
Those nipples, their breasts, that opulent clit
will soon slicken some unsuspecting other's week,
and you'll be small again, darned flat
by domestic pleasures, happy perhaps
as the catch that's unhooked and
tossed back to more familiar depths,
a snarl of silver wire caught in your lip.

MOTEL ART. DETAIL.

That girl who was twenty
and lay on her back beside me
weighed the merits of the two men
she supposed she loved.

"If only they could both be packed
into the same suitcase," she pouted,
moving slowly onto all fours,
"then I could lug them with me
wherever I went."

At which point, the wall clock paused
to accuse one second of tardiness.
The girl had short red hair,
narrow hips and—for one
misjudged moment—
the classical ease
of a body used to
expounding its bottom
to poised easels of pale oils.

A disappointment, then, when we failed
to make the piece into Art,
arranged as we were
like frank cuts of meat
in any common street's shop window.

Hitch was nervously pacing back and forth, saying it was awful and that he was going to cut it down for his television show. He was crazy. He didn't know what he had. "Wait a minute," I said, "I have some ideas. How about a score completely for strings? I used to be a violin player, you know".... Hitch was crazy then.... He didn't even want any music in the shower scene. Can you imagine that?

—BERNARD HERRMANN,
in conversation with Brian De Palma

APPRECIATING FEMALE FORM, 1960

Imagine she notices (her dress
already pooled around her ankles,
far below the body that stands stunned
in bra and black slip)—imagine
right then Janet Leigh notices
the peephole that points
to another mind.

Notices the crime, but for one more brief moment
(maybe a few seconds at most) does not
scramble for her dress. Instead,
she remains calm and still,
and feels the eye slide
down her neck like
a chip of ice, down
across her beating chest,
each breast a sudden gravity,
tipped with its hard, chilled nipple.

And perhaps Janet knows then
how a sensible room
with a little drilled secret
can make a woman more
famous, more awfully beautiful
than any other body
that has carelessly stripped itself
in supposed privacy.

ANECDOTE OF A SOUND GUY

In the recording studio,
Hitch sat quietly, eyes closed.
He might've been mistaken
for dead (each eyelid
drawn down
as if by a crime scene's
considerate first arrival)
but Hitch was alive—

listening, in fact, to
prop man Bob Bone
plunging butcher knives into
casabas, cantaloupes, honeydews:
a buffet of thick-skinned fruit
laid out on a long table
like an autopsy.

They were scoring a stabbing,
though I didn't know that
at the time. I stood off to the side
(having paused in the middle
of a coffee run, a hot cup
in each hand) watching
Hitch listen.

The fruit split, spat
seeds, bled juices, and yet
Bone's hand continued to stab,
stopping only when
the last melon had been
massacred. And you, too,

would've drawn breath
as Hitch opened his eyes
and declared calmly to a room,
"Casaba"—as a true master
selected with utter certainty
the sound for Janet Leigh's
skin breaking
ground in cabin one's
shower scene,

which incidentally
can now be heard more clearly
(drained like a tub
of Herrmann's strings)
courtesy of pristine DVD.

GOOD SCREAM

For Tuesday's event,
the role of Marion Crane was played
by Chicago-area receptionist
Sue Pelinski, fifty-five,
whose bloodcurdling shriek
won AMC's nationwide contest
to find the best *Psycho*
shower scene scream.
At the end of the mock stabbing,
Janet Leigh made her entrance
from behind a shower curtain—
for once on death's flip side—
and quipped to screaming Sue:
"You can stop that, now,"
and handed the receptionist a towel.

For the assembled news media
the two then screamed together.

For Leigh's scream launched
a thousand shower scenes
in which young curvy coeds
scrub away (working us into a lather)
oblivious to butcher knives our hearts
have cranked up like guillotines;

a thousand scenes, often shot in silence,
wanting only a good cynic
of a sound guy (played, say,
by John Travolta, circa *Blow Out*)
to record a single "good scream"
and stopper our coeds'
wide silent mouths.

How boring it must've been
for Brigitte Bardot's stand-in,
lying nude on her stomach,
hour after hour, as Godard
called for yet another close-up,
tilting the camera like a telescope
aimed at the heresy of two moons.

Perhaps she yawned, watching
gaffers move light around
a soundstage, arranging
the solar system that would
best illuminate Brigitte's bottom—
or perhaps leafed through *Life*,
smoking cigarettes.
It would've been cold,
her nipples stiff and irrefutable
as she lay waiting for the director's OK,
his ultimate approval of light.

Only then would the real Brigitte
finally appear on-set, stripping
even as she sauntered into the scene,
her clothes collecting lazily behind
like a sluggish comet's trail—and

only then would our stand-in
(now lingering just off-screen,
robe cinched) feel that sadness
particular to heavenly bodies
that have abandoned their orbits.
Sometimes the universe must adjust
itself to the arrival of stars.

THE QUESTION

(for Sonya Tomas)

After the dinner party, I walked
the daughter of the village beauty home,
bothered by the question of a first kiss.
The universe tracked neatly past, explaining itself
with simple examples: a community's
worth of hats in a haberdasher's window,
an empty Portuguese restaurant's poised tables,
a scrap of cloud caught in the branches above
like some starlet's abandoned boa.
No single thing—it seemed—could ever
properly be alone again.
The moon shone down, belonged
to all surfaces on which it laid its light,
and these surfaces—these leaves,
awnings and damp streets—belonged
back to the moon. We passed, finally,
a front yard's nativity scene, enjoying
its tackiness together, and, as her arm
slipped into mine, my feet a little ahead
of hers, hurrying us however imperceptibly
to our moment, the question resolved itself.

This first kiss on this cold street
could have once jailed Galileo
for the heavenly point it proves

but tonight, merely moves
two souls into steady revolution
around and about the warm
fixed fact of our brilliant lips.

A first kiss should be able to count
on silence, not the sax
that bleats holes through every date
like a little brother's blare, tagging—
nor the horn riff that pursues
Belmondo down Parisian rues
till he's *Breathless*.
Whenever we attempt front doors
warm strings swell around us,
rising like yeast, unstoppable,
music on which to gorge—or gag.
Even in shades, incognito,
in restaurants we've dimmed,
we're still not safe from
close-ups that close in
and constrict—our tongues scored
by every overcooked mouthful.

AUTUMN AT THE END OF *THE THIRD MAN*

What could Joseph possibly have said to Alida
if she'd paused to consider him
on her long way down the cemetery road?

Leaves left their trees and turned,
slow as Ferris wheels
against an Austrian sky, and though

Joseph was within seconds of his last
lonely cigarette, there were still (it seemed)
a thousand chances for Alida to pause,

for two near-lovers to gaze across
a grand moment at each other, Anton Karas'
zither score inoculating the season.

I used to be a violin player, you know.

—HERRMANN TO HITCH

ELEGY FOR JOSEF HASSID (1923-1950)

The violin's chin rest is a chopping
block. Upon it, you set your head, tilted just.
You close the eyes, raise the bow,
and Father's gushing applause cuts

out like a tap turned tight. Nothing left
for needles to plough but the pops
of one November's runout grooves.
These days, we press such silence with blues.

The fretboard
that trellises the guitar
guides fingers up and along its length

like roses.
But not the violin,
Father stresses. The violin is fretless—

strings climb
its smooth neck like arteries
bearing bursts of blood up to a thought.

A violinist's fingers,
Father stresses, must therefore train
to pursue, like medics, the jump of a pulse.

RICKY'S TWIN BED ADDRESSES LUCY'S

Unlike you and me (whose sheets
are well-tucked every morning)
love never gets made in
this New York City apartment.

Once, you might've expected my Cuban
hot-blooded and rough with women.
Fair enough. I expected your redhead,
usually so crazy with schemes and ploys,

to suggest new positions now and then,
to keep up on the latest trends
in physical love, the novel way
they're doing it in Paris this season.

You and me, though, are never slid
together, and the excruciating gap
between us remains carefully televised
fact, keeping America calm.

A minor character in any caress, the pinky's
nevertheless responsible for Q, A and Z,
plus dutifully brings up the rear of every handshake.
Children swear by it, an authority to pacify playgrounds,
and though small, it adds itself to every effort
like a child aiding adults. Imagine, then,
all the gestures Father's finger will never join,
kisses left unblown upon the awkward palm,
one thousand waves goodbye maimed again
and again, falling onto the dusty floor of the mine.
The absent finger phantoms the hand
but at least it's his bowing hand—
a violin, after all, can still be bowed by nine.

"Violinist's fingers," Father sighs,
squeezing my left hand with his right
as we watch *Humoresque* on TV—sighs
because these fingers I've fed to
handshakes, keyboards and
the rough gullets of work gloves
will never find first position now—
never place the pulse on an ebony neck.
Meanwhile, onscreen, John Garfield plays
not one note either. A camera trick cuts him
at the wrists, cuts to Isaac Stern's hands
on close-up. And what I'd give up
for an edit of my own, for a virtuoso
to glove me with grace—for *my* stolen solos
to gush from the grilles of radios,
to flood bedrooms and buoy stars
like Joan Crawford far
out into the ocean.

Ideally, the heart would weigh no more
than Audrey Hepburn's right hand
in *Wait Until Dark.*
Cast as blind, Audrey
gropes her graceful way
through this '67 thriller,
but it's the digits that pilfer
the show—five fingers
light as canaries as they light
on ledges, tables, countertops:
a mineshaft's memorized textures.
Dispatched into darkness,
each manicured fingertip can
teach hearts how to proceed with care,
to parse light fixtures from lovers—
banisters against which we brace—
how, most of all, to hold fast.
But your chest traps a child's fist,
beating to get out, to get its fingers into
everything. If only love *was,*
as we like to lament, blind.

CLEANING KILL IN THE KITCHEN AT MIDNIGHT, FATHER MADE A GOOD POINT

He noticed me on my way to bed,
holding his violin by the neck
as if it was fresh game, and said,

"She always leaves you in autumn,"

while outside, through the window
through which Bach (cooked by bow)
would later waft, night seasoned its sky
with eighth notes in negative.

And after all, only Whitman and Crane and Williams, of the American poets, are better than the movies.

—Frank O'Hara

AVA GARDNER RESPONDS TO "AVA GARDNER REINCARNATED AS A MAGNOLIA" BY MARGARET ATWOOD

Restore me to life, sure, but not
potted in poetry. (If anything, I
was sunlight, and broads like you
the foliage, straining on your stalks
to sop me up.) Honey, plant *yourself*.
Peddle museums on the subway, make
that buck. You, too, would take
pool tables over coffins.

THE DAY FRANK O'HARA DIED. DETAIL.

Blood streaks the sand like paint
from Pollock's brush, but no,
the beach won't hang. Won't show.
Still, let your wet clouds set
and burr the sky's blue fibre—
canvas only religion can stretch.
Once dry, render rocks, gulls,
our poet wheezing on barren ground.
Tweeze not one grain of quartz
from his left eyebrow. (The dune buggy
seems a surreal touch, yes,
but Frank would've loved
the detail.) Compose, then,
what really happens to men.
You have licence to the grim,
de Kooning's duty to ugly edges.
You have life left.

FOR WELDON KEES AS HE TEETERS

Periodically, poetic licence places you
on the Golden Gate Bridge, July 18, 1955—a Monday.
In fact, one microfilmed page of *The New York Times*
puts your last breaths of bay air at sixty-two degrees.
A fine day to jump, then. The breeze clawed like children,
daughters you didn't conceive in closing couplets.

And though biography confirms you left keys
dangling in the ignition—your Plymouth Savoy abandoned nearby—
I cannot allow you a key chain, nor imagine
its novelty, what cheeky slogan it might assert.
No document records whether you shaved that morning
but I've decided your moustache remains firmly fixed.

Let's assume seagulls perched on piling.
Let's suppose sunlight strumming the cables
discouraged you, or at least held your gaze
for a metaphor or two. We'll not take the temperature
of water—cold will be our conclusion.

For a few years in the '50s—in the den of what,
from outside, would've resembled
just another white stucco bungalow,
one of thousands post-war planning snapped
into LA's great suburban grids—

you could sit on Bela Lugosi's sofa and,
if Halloween, watch the one he was known for,
Dracula, while the old eccentric
sat beside in cape and collar,
demonstrating those double-jointed onscreen fingers
famed, like Hungarian stresses, for their snap.

There, on that sofa—brooded over
by a portrait of Dracula, posed for
too many years ago—you could learn
the leathery stage name, 'Bela Lugosi,'
actually sheathed a dagger of serrated syllables:
'Béla Ferenc Dezsõ Blaskó,'
and his sleeves: an addict's arms, pocked
as the necks his alter ego sucked.

Necks. *Vimen*. Vampira's *jugs*.

Brooded over, under an old man's wing,
you, too, could master *vimen* who
prefairred the tradeetional monstairrs to
atomic age mutations.
(*Take hairr to see* Dracula, he'd advise,
not giant grasshoppers.)

In the '50s, in a den—before decades battling
methadone and morphine
bled the body, propped by your side, dry
of its Bela—you could crush
Hollywood's thinning legend to your chest
like an aged poster bleached of its dyes;
promise his memorabilia would always outsell Karloff's;
see what love, transfused, might Colorize.

Yes, I died in *The Winter's Tale*,
left life in III, iii—
the part where Will
loosed his bear upon me.
That's no way to go: chased off
stage and into wilderness,
pursued by your plot
and its appetite.

Usually, though, Will
arranged artful exits.
This, after all, is the quill
who dipped Ophelia feather-first
into her inky brook; the Will
that dressed Desdemona for bed,
eased her onto crisp white sheets and
even lit a wick (as if ticking
a syllable's stress) before cueing
Othello's hands.

I would've preferred grace,
my death soluble, stirred
into a cup. I could've clutched
my chest like Gertrude,

swooning out of life
and into excellence.

But I would've also approved
a performance of swords
on the battlefield,
my body opened expertly
and emptied, my blood
spread across the turf
like a red banner.

Well, Will
trampled a history of men
into his battlefields, men
of nobility, pitched from saddles,
limbs end-stopped against axes.
Hell, even Macbeth's head—
edited offstage—was later
returned to the scene and
raised like a toast.

I, too, wanted to be—ah, *To be*—
sent off with a sentence of poetry,
thirty or so words set
between my lips like teeth:
smooth durable syllables
that might've survived
the body's brevity.

Look, the role of Antigonus
isn't with*out* honour.
I provided the feast, after all,
kept a bear fed for
centuries, in print and onstage.

But ultimately, I passed
in pieces through an animal, eased
out with the excrement
and left, like all droppings,
uncollected behind the curtain.

ON BEHALF OF ALL INSTRUCTIVE IMAGES

What became of the red wheelbarrow
once the thoughtful doctor
had made his point (a good one
and worth the ink in all those anthologies)?

Well, at best, the glaze of rainwater dried
and helped restore a cloud to the sky,
though all white chickens surely perished—
perhaps in a local kitchen, the chafed
hands of wives and daughters
wringing for dinner.

The wheelbarrow, we hope, let down
none of its dependents. It's wished well
by decades of readers. It may still
even move earth along in modest loads
somewhere, and if ever junked, road-
side, we expect any just
and competent antique dealer
(passing by happy coincidence)
will have the good sense to intervene...

AS WE DOLLY BACK

(for Maurice Darantiere)

From a single dot
Joyce instructed one French printer
to set near the end of *Ulysses*
(just below "Where?" and
right before Molly)
much has been wrung.
And though some editions
print a circle (●) and
others, a square (■)
often, whatever it is
is not even there,
or simply ignored like
the florid typographer's mark
that blooms in the crack
between Victorian chapters
(the sidewalk weed
reading eyes skip).
But no matter how menstrual
Molly may have been,
budding filmmakers like myself
still don't spot a period
but, rather, an Earth
glimpsed from great distance
as we dolly back:

an Earth eclipsed by ink,
so slippery, so very vast
only typesetters (only you,
Maurice) could fix it fast.

In the light proposed by an overhead window,
the very same species of smile that
bothered da Vinci to his brushes
now made a mystery of Orson's face.

A novelist, stunned by this tryst of the lips,
called out across the slick cobblestones,
but Orson's shadow slid freely away
along the crumbling walls like
fresco excused from its plaster.

ON-SET IN HADES, 1911

Then the crowd
dissolved its affiliation

and the delicate faces blew off
their bough and continued
on through the station

of the metro, while not one soul
realized what it had just added to the world
by simply pausing on a platform
among a small sampling
of photogenic Parisians.

The movies were simply awful, but Ezra loved them. He'd sit up in the gallery with a cowboy hat on and his feet up on the rail, eating peanuts, roaring with laughter.

—JAMES LAUGHLIN

RIFIFI

Just before FIN, the young French boy
fidgeting next to you in the front seat
aims his plastic pistol at your temple.
The cowboy hat and toy spurs signal
an American West that's gone wild
in his head, and then his lips explode:
a sibilant killing sound that denotes your death.

Unlike you, this boy's healthy,
chambered with youth,
blowing imagined curls of smoke off
the barrel's Chinese-made tip.
His lungs are little pink cobras
of country air, while you cough
(not good at playing dead) and think:
I could use a trip to the country
or a good comb run through my hair.

It's still your duty, though, to get this child
home, and so you drive faster, swerving
recklessly through Paris, your hands gripping
both sides of the steering wheel
as if wringing lapels, giving
some deadbeat a good scare.

Know, first, this hand holds your treat.

Sniff, then, no bitch's bottom tonight.

Instead, be light on those paws. Be the cloud I have combed you into. Be your best white.

If you must bark, bark backward into your mind, and leave it there, echoing.

Yes, watch the Japanese judge with scrutiny. Admire the soft tips of his delicious fingers as they lift that Doberman's lips. Admire, too, the white teeth, brushed and stacked like a warning of skulls before some village gate (remember *Apocalypse Now?*), but then admire the Doberman's restraint. If he can resist a bite, so can you.

Ignore, further, all Schnauzers, and be glad you are no Sheepdog.

Know, above all, pride.

Bear the fact of your beauty upon your hind legs as you prance into hearts and imaginations.

At the Westminster Dog Show, applauding hands make a thunder you cannot and will not fear, and, when in doubt, repeat merely what is true:

"This is not grass, but it will have to do."

AS SHE LAY IN HER BATHTUB,
HOLDING A FLUTE OF WINE

Miss P—'s voice often returned to
details of her first love the way

a line of cursive must sometimes
pause in its progress to dote upon

undotted 'i's, or loop back gracefully,
spawning 'o's and 'l's—the way

great scenes rewind again and
again when we aim our remotes.

Usually, a Newfoundland dog,
unhappy on damp bathroom floor,

would nevertheless wait patiently
for the narrative to knot itself.

A dying man is apt
to be ambiguous,
to recall an odd, unsatisfying
detail that he may then
utter mysteriously
as prelude, a trailer
for the soul.

He shatters a snow
globe because he can—
the dying are entitled,
after all, to release
little blizzards from their
swirling sentence—

and he expects
the afterlife to privilege
that clean tint of white
particular to his
industrious nurse's
simple smock.

(Audio Commentary

Of course,
long before
the DVD format,
Eliot invented
the first Modern
audio commentary
track, fitting
The Waste Land
with notes no
more useful
than a director's
disembodied voice
explaining
just where exactly
he found
his snow globe,
and why
he wanted it to slip
from fingers,
to shatter
just so.)

Over time, his chin doubled, his face fattened,
his every word wheezed its way out.
He found himself in lurid settings—
throttling stock villains while
drugged Janet Leigh lay nearby,
innocent as a motel Bible.
(Even then, she knew her niche.)

Earlier, he'd held a god's office,
presiding over three famous minutes
of film, a single tracking shot
that elaborated the limits of his universe:
parked car, street, explosion—
but no more such ambition.

By the end, he struggled merely to picture
the shape and make of a cane
that might steady his hobbled thoughts,
and wanted very badly to slap the Mexican clean
off Charlton Heston's bronzed face.
Marlene assessed a mess, honey.

Washing bloody hands in water
choked with garbage, Orson accepted irony.
Made popular his art. He longed, finally,
to sit down to a hot bowl of chili,
set lovingly before him by his dreamed-of gypsy.

TROUTY

(for Richard Teleky)

In old movies, one went by train
and could expect blondes to coin
comic adjectives. Of course,
dining compartments don't serve
Eva Marie Saint's sort anymore—
a delicacy done away with.
And cameras no longer cut to
the locomotive penetrating its tunnel.
(Imaginations could manage
coitus back then, and lovers
enjoyed an abolished privacy,
their hearts wheeling like crop-dusters
over wide empty vistas.)

Cut the nostalgia, I tell myself.
So what if women no longer
think things "trouty" or hang
like great lines from the stone lips
of Rushmore's presidents?—I *want*
to tell myself, but don't. No,
I'll mute such snipes and—
as two lovers stow themselves
with the overhead luggage—wonder
only if I should've opted for wider screens.

No finis to the film unless
The ending is your own.

—WELDON KEES

NOTES

Hugh Kenner's quote can be found in his book, *The Pound Era* (Los Angeles: University of California Press).

August Kleinzahler's lines are drawn from his poem, "An Englishman Abroad," which can be found in *The Strange Hours Travelers Keep* (New York: FSG).

Bernard Herrmann's quote can be found in Stephen Rebello's *Alfred Hitchcock and the Making of* Psycho (New York: Dembner Books). Rebello's book also inspired the poem, "Anecdote of a Sound Guy."

Minus edits and additions, the first two stanzas of "Good Scream" largely constitute found poetry—text that has been extracted and relined from an article, "Actress Janet Leigh Returns to Bates Motel," appearing online in the *Shanghai Star* (August 4, 2000).

Frank O'Hara's quote can be found in *The Collected Poems of Frank O'Hara* (New York: Knopf).

James Laughlin's quote can be found in Humphrey Carpenter's *A Serious Character: The Life of Ezra Pound* (Boston: Houghton Mifflin).

Weldon Kees' lines are drawn from his poem, "Subtitle," which can be found in *The Collected Poems of Weldon Kees* (Lincoln: University of Nebraska Press).

ACKNOWLEDGMENTS

Special thanks to my mentor, Richard Teleky, without whose guidance many of these poems simply wouldn't exist, and to Sonya Tomas for her love and support.

Thanks also to my family, Shirley, Ciprian and Natalie Guriel; Priscila Uppal for helping this book find its shape; Barry Callaghan and the Ontario Arts Council, respectively, for generous support; Evan Jones, Dimitri Nasrallah, and Paul Stanley for helpful readings; Joe Paczuski for a wonderful photograph; the expert eye of Belal Khallad for identifying the car in *Whatever Happened to Baby Jane?*; and Heather Pantrey and Ann Birch for their crucial encouragement many years ago.

Morency, Pierre A SEASON FOR BIRDS Selected Poems (1990); THE EYE IS AN EAGLE (1992) • Moriarity, Michael THE GIFT OF STERN ANGELS (1997) • Morley, David MANDELSTAM VARIATIONS (1993) • Moses, Daniel David THE INDIAN MEDICINE SHOWS Two One-Act Plays (1995, 2002); BIG BUCK CITY: A Play In Two Acts (1998); BRÉBEUF'S GHOST (2000); SIXTEEN JESUSES (2000); PURSUED BY A BEAR (2005) • Murray, George CAROUSEL A Book of Second Thoughts (2000) • Musgrave, Susan THE EMBALMER'S ART Selected Poems 1970-1985 (1991) • Nečakov, Lillian HAT TRICK (1998) • Nemiroff, Daniel NASTY, SHORT AND BRUTAL (2004) • Nepveu, Pierre ROMANS-FLEUVES (1998) • Neruda, Pablo 100 LOVE SONNETS (2004) • Oates, Joyce Carol JOYCE CAROL OATES IN EXILE (1990) • Ouellette, Fernand WELLS OF LIGHT Selected Poems 1955-1981 (1989) • Outram, Richard SELECTED POEMS 1960-1980 (1984) • Owen, Catherine SOMATIC The Life and Work of Egon Shiele (1998) • Pasolini, Pier Paolo POETRY (1991) • Pasternak, Boris MY SISTER-LIFE (1989) • Paterson, Mark OTHER PEOPLE'S SHOWERS (2003) • Pavlović, Miodrag LINKS (1989); SINGING AT THE WHIRLPOOL (1983); A VOICE LOCKED IN STONE (1985) • Pelchat, Jean THE AFTERLIFE OF VINCENT VAN GOGH (2001) • Plater, Max WINTER FIRES (1998) • Prewett, Frank SELECTED POEMS OF FRANK PREWETT (1987) • Quarrina, Odida T. ALL THINGS CONSIDERED: CAN WE LIVE TOGETHER (1996) • Reeves, John ABOUT FACE (1990); INCONTRO Where Italy and Canada Meet (1996) • Rhenisch, Harold FUSION (1999) • Riel, Louis SELECTED POETRY OF LOUIS RIEL (1993) • Roberts, Charles G.D. KINDRED OF THE WILD (2001) • Rogel, Stan PERSONATIONS (1997) • Rogers, Linda LOVE IN THE RAINFOREST New and Selected Poetry (1995) • Ronald, William THE PRIME MINISTERS (1983) • Rooke, Leon OH! TWENTY-SEVEN STORIES (1997); WHO GOES THERE (1998) • Rosenblatt, Joe SNAKE OIL Exile Editions Number 8 (1978); THE SLEEPING LADY (1979); ESCAPE FROM THE GLUE FACTORY A Memoir of a Paranormal Toronto Childhood in the Late Forties (1985, 1987); THE KISSING GOLDFISH OF SIAM (1989); THE JOE ROSENBLATT READER (1995); A TENTACLED MOTHER (Piscatorially Perverse Sonnets (1995); PARROT FEVER (2002) • Ross, W.W.E. IRREALITIES, SONNETS & LACONICS (2003) • Rubess, Banuta BOOM, BABY, BOOM! A Jazz Play (1995); HEAD IN A BAG (1995); SMOKE DAMAGE (1995) • Sabines, Jaime WEEKLY DIARY AND POEMS IN PROSE & ADAM AND EVE (2004) • Safarik, Allan BIRD WRITER'S HANDBOOK (2002) • Schädlich, Hans Joachim EASTWEST BERLIN (1992) • Schafer, R. Murray ARIADNE/Exile Editions Number 7 (1977) • Shelly, Nadine BAREBACKED WITH RAIN (1990) • Shreve, Sandy SUDDENLY, SO MUCH (2005) • Simonsuuri, Kirsti BOY-DEVIL (1992) • Slavicek, Milivoj SILENT DOORS Selected Poems (1988) • Soljan, Antun THE STONE THROWER & OTHER POEMS Selected Poems (1990) • Somers, Harry KYRIE Exile Editions Number 4 (1976) • Strimas, Meaghan JUNKMAN'S DAUGHTER (2004) • Summerhayes, Don MYSTORY (1997); THIS OLD MAN RECLINES ON THE FIELD OF HEAVEN Poems 1979-1999 (2000) • Tomlinson, Charles SELECTED POEMS (1989) • Tarnapolsky, Damian LANZMAN and Other Stories (2006) • Tremblay, Michel THE GUID SISTERS (1988) • Tutunjian, Jirair CONVENT OF CYPRESSES, A HILL OF BONES (2001) • Ukrainetz, Elizabeth MINOR ASSUMPTIONS (1994) • Ungaretti, Giuseppe A MAJOR SELECTION OF THE POETRY OF GIUSEPPE UNGARETTI (1997) • Uppal, Priscila HOW TO DRAW BLOOD FROM A STONE (1998); CONFESSIONS OF A FERTILITY EXPERT (1999); PRETENDING TO DIE (2001); LIVE COVERAGE (2003); ONTOLOGICAL NECESSITIES (2006) • Varnai, Paul (As Editor) HUNGARIAN SHORT STORIES (1983) • Virgo, Seán WHITE LIES & OTHER FICTIONS (1980); SELAKHI (1987); WHITE LIES & OTHER FICTIONS, PLUS TWO (1989); WORMWOOD Fictions (1989); SELECTED POEMS (1989); WAKING IN EDEN (1990); BEGGING QUESTIONS (2006) • Vorobyov, Mykola WILD DOG ROSE MOON (1992) • Waits, Death MY TONGUE, MY TEETH, YOUR VOICE (1992); THE EARTH IS A WITCH, THE WITCH IS A SAINT, THE SAINT IS APPLAUSE (1994); 62 ROCK VIDEOS for songs that will never exist (1996) • Wevill, David OTHER NAMES FOR THE HEART New and Selected Poems 1964-1984 (1985); FIGURE OF EIGHT New Poems and Selected Translations (1987); CHILD EATING SNOW (1994); SOLO WITH GRAZING DEER (2001) • Wilkinson, Anne THE POETRY OF ANNE WILKINSON And a Prose Memoir (1990) • Wilks, Claire Runnin DRAWINGS/Exile Editions Number 1 (1975) • Wilks, Claire Weissman THE MAGIC BOX: The Eccentric Genius of Hannah Mayard, Photographer 1834-1918 (1980); TWO OF US TOGETHER, EACH OF US ALONE (1982); HILLMOTHER (1983); I KNOW NOT WHY THE ROSES BLOOM Drawings Lithographs Sculpture 1982-1986 (1986); IN THE WHITE HOTEL With Poems by D.M. Thomas (1991) • Werup, Jacques THE TIME IN MALMO ON THE EARTH (1989) • Yemec, Daria Tatianna MY MOTHER'S FLOWERS With Poems by G.M. Yemec (1991) • Zeifman, Stephen THE FAMILY MAN (1998); THE GOOD FRIEND (2000); THE BEN CALDER STORY (2005) • Zeller, Ludwig TO SAW THE BELOVED TO PIECES ONLY WHEN NECESSARY (1990); TOTEM WOMEN (1993) • Zend, Robert OAB VOLUME ONE (1983); OAB VOLUME TWO (1985) • Ziedonis, Imants FLOWERS OF ICE (1987) • Zigaina, Giuseppe PASOLINI Between Enigma and Prophecy (1990) • Zolf, Larry ZOLF (1999) *** THE DARKHORSE SERIES Harding, John HARM-LESS VICTORIES Number One (1993) • Ukrainetz, Elizabeth BABY I LOVE YOU Number Two (1993) • Dodic, N.J. ALL THE WAY TO ACELDAMA Number Three (1993) • Schertzer, Mike SHORT FILMS OF THE 14TH CENTURY Number Four (1994) • O'Leary, Sara WISH YOU WERE HERE Number Five (1994) • Kackley, Dawn EVEN THIS IS LOVE Number Six (1995) • Kinski, Edward THE ESCALADE Number Seven (1996) • Muir, Fran COMING TO BONE Number Eight (1997) • Hunter, Sarah CORE REALITY Number Nine (1999) • Green, Kristi-Ly NITS Number Ten (2000) • Zeifman, Stephen PERIPHERAL VISION Number Eleven (2002) *** PIGAS SERIES REPRINTS Lane, Patrick/No. 17 MORTAL REMAINS (1999) • MacEwen, Gwendolyn/No. 18 POETRY OF GWENDOLYN MACEWEN Volume One The Early Years (1993) • MacEwen, Gwendolyn/No. 19 POETRY OF GWENDOLYN MACEWEN Volume Two The Later Years (1994) • Bessette, Gérard/No. 20 NOT FOR EVERY EYE (1994) • Annesley, David/No. 21 THE ANNESLEY DRAWINGS (1980) • Clarke, Austin/No. 23. THERE ARE NO ELDERS (2000) • Prewett, Frank/No. 24 SELECTED POEMS OF FRANK PREWETT (2000) • Riel, Louis/No. 25 SELECTED POETRY OF LOUIS RIEL (2000) • McGee, Thomas D'Arcy/No. 26 SELECTED VERSE OF THOMAS D'ARCY McGEE (2000) • Salivarova, Zdena/No. 27 ASHES, ASHES, ALL FALL DOWN (2000) • Brault, Jacques/No. 29 FRAGILE MOMENTS (2000) • Tremblay, Michel/No. 31 THE GUID SISTERS A translation of Les Belles-Soeurs into modern Scots (2000) • Hénault, Gilles/No. 33 SIGNALS FOR SEERS (2000) • Amichai, Yehuda/No. 35 TRAVELS (2001) • Amprimoz, Alexandre/No. 37 TOO MANY POPES (2001) • Rosenblatt, Joe/No.39 THE SLEEPING LADY (2001) • Brault, Jacques/No. 41 ON THE ROAD NO MORE (2001) • Virgo, Seán/No. 43 THROUGH THE EYES OF A CAT (2001) • Ouellette, Fernand/No. 45 WELLS OF LIGHT Selected Poems (2003) • Beaulieu, Michel/No. 47 SPELLS OF FURY (2003) • Brett, Brian/No. 49 UPROAR'S YOUR ONLY MUSIC (2006) • Marteau, Robert/No. 51 PIG-SKINNING (2006) *** EXILE EDUCATIONAL SERIES Callaghan, Morley/No. 1 THAT SUMMER IN PARIS (2006) • Bacque, James/No. 2 CRIMES AND MERCIES (2006) • Blais, Marie-Claire/No. 3 NIGHTS IN THE UNDERGROUND (2006) • Blais, Marie-Claire/No. 4 DEAF TO THE CITY (2006)

Exile Editions

info@exileeditions.com

www.ExileEditions.com

publishers of singular
fiction, poetry, drama, photography and art
since 1976